AMICUS ILLUSTRATED • AMICUS INK

DO YOU REALLY WANT TO MEET
A MOOSE?

WRITTEN BY CARI MEISTER   ILLUSTRATED BY DANIELE FABBRI

Amicus Illustrated and Amicus Ink
are imprints of Amicus
P.O. Box 1329
Mankato, MN 56002
www.amicuspublishing.us

Library of Congress Cataloging-in-Publication Data
Meister, Cari, author.
 Do you really want to meet a moose? / Cari Meister ;
illustrated by Daniele Fabbri.
    pages cm. — (Do you really want to meet...?)
 Summary: "A child goes on an adventure in a
national park, learns how to track moose in the
wild, and learns not to bother a baby moose with its
mother"— Provided by publisher.
 Audience: K to grade 3.
 ISBN 978-1-60753-736-6 (library binding)
 ISBN 978-1-60753-840-0 (ebook)
 ISBN 978-1-68152-010-0 (paperback)
 1. Moose—Juvenile literature. 2. Canada—Juvenile
literature. I. Fabbri, Daniele, 1978– illustrator. II. Title.
 QL737.U55M372 2016
 599.65'7—dc23   2014036505

Editor   Rebecca Glaser
Designer   Kathleen Petelinsek

Printed in the United States of America at
Corporate Graphics in North Mankato, Minnesota.

HC 10 9 8 7 6 5 4 3 2 1
PB 10 9 8 7 6 5 4 3 2 1

ABOUT THE AUTHOR

Cari Meister is the author of more than 120 books for
children, including the *Tiny* (Penguin Books for Young
Readers) series and *Snow White and the Seven Dogs*
(Scholastic, 2014). She lives in Evergreen, Colorado, with
her husband John, four sons, one horse, and one dog.
You can visit Cari online at *www.carimeister.com*.

ABOUT THE ILLUSTRATOR

Daniele Fabbri was born in Ravenna, Italy, in 1978. He
graduated from Istituto Europeo di Design in Milan, Italy,
and started his career as a cartoon animator, storyboarder,
and background designer for animated series. He has
worked as a freelance illustrator since 2003, collaborating
with international publishers and advertising agencies.

So you say you want to meet a moose.
Not here, in the visitor center, but in the wild?

Moose *do* look funny, but did you know they can be deadly? Moose kill more people in Canada than grizzly bears do!

Do you still *really* want to meet a moose?

Okay. There's an outfitter down the road that offers moose tours. The guides know just where to look for wild moose. On the way, watch for moose on the road. They can do some pretty serious damage to a moving car.

Here we are! Put on your life jacket so
you can ride the pontoon boat. Moose
were spotted across the lake this morning.

Did you know that moose are great swimmers? They swim to cool down, escape from predators (like bears and wolves), and to get away from pesky mosquitos. WHOA! Look at those bubbles.

A MOOSE!

He's big, and a little scary, but he doesn't even have upper front teeth!

Moose are vegetarians. They eat water lilies, underwater plants, twigs and bark, and other plants.

What? You want to see *another* moose? We can try to track a moose in the woods. Follow the guide. Look for piles of moose scat, or as most people say, poop.

Look for lay marks, too. Moose are massive
animals—some weigh up to 1,800 pounds (820 kg).
When they lie down, they leave marks in the grass.

Don't forget to check out the trees. When male moose grow new antlers (which they do every spring), they are covered in fuzz. They scrape the fuzz off by rubbing their antlers on trees. It leaves big marks.

Be sure to check for tracks. Moose hoof prints
are about 5 to 7 inches long (13–18 cm).
They are pointed and split in two halves.

Oh look! A baby moose!
Baby moose, like their parents,
have big heads, large hooves,
and humps on their backs.

The poor little guy seems lost. Maybe he needs help finding his mama. Should you help him?

Absolutely not! Here comes mama and she is NOT happy you are admiring her baby. When faced with an angry moose in the wild, DO NOT RUN!

Don't let a moose's long, thin legs fool you. Moose can run up
to 35 miles per hour (55 km/h)—way faster than you!
If you are faced with an angry moose, CLIMB A TREE!

While you are waiting for the angry moose to mosey away, be sure to check out the view.

You might even be lucky enough to spot some other moose from up there!

WHERE DO MOOSE LIVE?

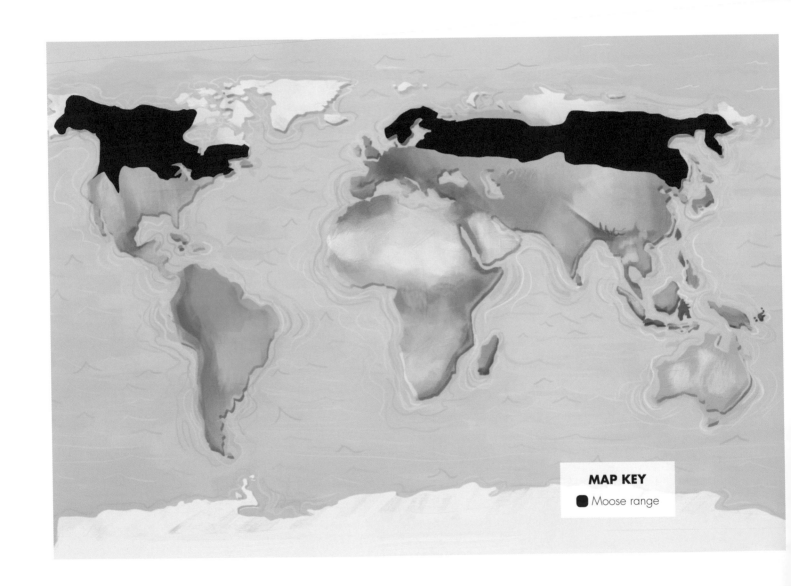

MAP KEY

● Moose range

GLOSSARY

antlers The large, branching structures that grow on a male moose's head.

hoof The hard part of a moose's foot.

outfitter A business that brings people into the wilderness to explore nature.

pontoon A type of platform boat.

predator An animal that hunts and eats other animals.

scat Animal poop.

READ MORE

Carr, Aaron. *Moose*. New York: AV2 by Weigl, 2014.

Owen, Ruth. **Moose**. New York: Windmill Books, 2014.

Riggs, Kate. **Moose**. Amazing Animals. Mankato, Minn.: Creative Education, 2012.

Schuetz, Kristin. **Moose**. Backyard Wildlife. Minneapolis: Bellwether Media, 2014.

WEBSITES

Moose | Arkive
www.arkive.org/moose/alces-americanus/
Watch videos of moose in the wild.

The Moose—Canadian Animals
www.aitc.sk.ca/saskschools/animals/moose.html
Visit this site to research facts about moose.

Ranger Rick: Mighty Moose
www.nwf.org/kids/ranger-rick/animals/mammals/moose.aspx
Read about moose, see photos, and learn some moose jokes.

Yellowstone National Park: Moose
www.nps.gov/yell/naturescience/moose.htm
Read about the moose that live in this park and find out where to see them.

Every effort has been made to ensure that these websites are appropriate for children. However, because of the nature of the Internet, it is impossible to guarantee that these sites will remain active indefinitely or that their contents will not be altered.